Decomposers
Earth's Clean-up Crew

Jill Bryant

Decomposers: Earth's Clean-up Crew

Text: Jill Bryant
Publishers: Tania Mazzeo and Eliza Webb
Series consultant: Amanda Sutera
    Hands on Heads Consulting
Editor: Jarrah Moore
Project editor: Annabel Smith
Designer: Leigh Ashforth
Project designer: Danielle Maccarone
Permissions researcher: Liz McShane
Production controller: Renee Tome

Acknowledgements
We would like to thank the following for permission to reproduce
copyright material:

Front cover: iStock.com/Brett_Hondow; pp. 1, 14: Shutterstock.
com/Rainer Fuhrmann; p. 4 (top): iStock.com/Orbon Alija, (bottom):
iStock.com/Xsandra; p. 5: iStock.com/GENETTICA; p. 6 (top): Science Photo
Library/Eye of Science, (bottom): Science Photo Library/Dennis Kunkel
Microscopy; p. 7 (top): Shutterstock.com/mynewturtle, (bottom):
Shutterstock.com/sruilk; p. 8 (main): Shutterstock.com/Nick N A, (inset):
Science Photo Library/Culture/Gregory S.; p. 9 (top): Alamy Stock
Photo/blickwinkel, (bottom): Fairfax Syndication/Wayne Taylor; p. 10 (top):
iStock.com/rai, (bottom): iStock.com/Andreas Häuslbetz; p. 11 (top):
iStock.com/MirasWonderland, (bottom): Alamy Stock Photo/The Natural
History Museum; pp. 12 (top left), 24: Shutterstock.com/Paulrommer SL;
p. 12 (top right): iStock.com/maryolyna, (bottom): iStock.
com/FrankRamspott; p. 13 (top left): Alamy Stock Photo/Custom Life
Science Images, (top right): iStock.com/Edward Bibbey, (bottom): iStock.
com/Nynke van Holten; p. 15 (top): iStock.com/ljphoto7, (bottom): Nature
in Stock/Minden Pictures/Konrad Wothe; p. 16 (left): Alamy Stock
Photo/Nigel Cattlin, (right): naturepl.com/Solvin Zankl; p. 17 (left): Science
Photo Library/Wim Van Egmond, (right): Science Photo Library/Eye of
Science; p. 18: Shutterstock.com/GraphicsRF.com; p. 19: naturepl.
com/Jose B. Ruiz; p. 20 (measuring cup): Getty Images/Science Photo
Library; pp. 20–22: Lindsay Edwards Photography © Cengage Learning
Australia; p. 23: iStock.com/Imagesines; back cover (top): iStock.com/rai,
(bottom): Shutterstock.com/Nick N A.

Every effort has been made to trace and acknowledge copyright.
However, if any infringement has occurred, the publishers tender their
apologies and invite the copyright holders to contact them.

NovaStar

Text © 2024 Cengage Learning Australia Pty Limited

ISBN 978 0 17 033428 0

Cengage Learning Australia
Level 5, 80 Dorcas Street
Southbank VIC 3006 Australia
Phone: 1300 790 853
Email: aust.nelsonprimary@cengage.com

For learning solutions, visit cengage.com.au

Printed in China by 1010 Printing International Ltd
1 2 3 4 5 6 7 28 27 26 25 24

*Nelson acknowledges the Traditional Owners and Custodians
of the lands of all First Nations Peoples. We pay respect
to Elders past and present, and extend that respect to
all First Nations Peoples today.*

Contents

Changing Scraps into Healthy Soil

Carrot peels, onion skins and apple cores are some of the scraps that can be left over from cooking or baking. In fact, lots of the **waste** made in kitchens contains parts of vegetables and fruits.

Many families keep a small bin in the kitchen for food waste.

Leftover scraps don't have to be wasted!

A good place to toss this waste is into a **compost heap**. When waste is added to a compost heap, the waste **rots**. Over time, it turns into dark, **rich** soil, which helps plants to grow.

How does this happen? With the help of decomposers, of course!

Decomposers are living things that help change waste into healthy soil. Some are really small. Others are so tiny, humans can't even see them!

When food waste is put into a compost heap, decomposers break it down.

Bacteria and Fungi

The tiniest decomposers are **bacteria**. They are microscopic, meaning scientists need microscopes to see them. Bacteria are the smallest of all life forms. There are around 10 000 different kinds of bacteria.

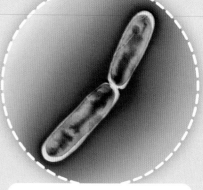

bacteria seen through a microscope

Fungi (say: *fun-gee*) are not plants or animals. Instead, they are their own group of living things. There are about 72 000 different kinds of fungi. Like bacteria, fungi are found in soil, air and even inside the human body.

tiny fungi seen through a microscope

In compost heaps, bacteria and microscopic fungi help break down waste. Fungi often gobble up the things bacteria can't eat. Together, bacteria and fungi take in **nutrients** that are found in dead plants. Then they leave behind their own waste, which puts lots of this good stuff back into the soil. In this way, they recycle important nutrients!

As the waste rots, the compost heap gets warmer. Then, other larger fungi such as mushrooms and **moulds** start to grow. Mushrooms and moulds feed on rotting plants that are full of nutrients.

fungi growing in a compost heap

moulds growing on food

More About Bacteria and Fungi

→ Farmers sometimes add special bacteria to soil to help plants grow.

→ Some medicines that save lives are made from fungi.

Earthworms

Earthworms are invertebrates – animals that don't have a backbone. In fact, they don't have any bones at all! Earthworms are also called **segmented** worms. Their long, narrow bodies are made up of many sections, or segments.

Earthworms can be pink, purple, red or brown. They have strong muscles for pushing through soil. Earthworms breathe through their **moist** skin. They only use their small mouths to eat dead leaves and rotting plants. They also eat dead insects. This is helpful for cleaning up the surface of soil.

Parts of an Earthworm

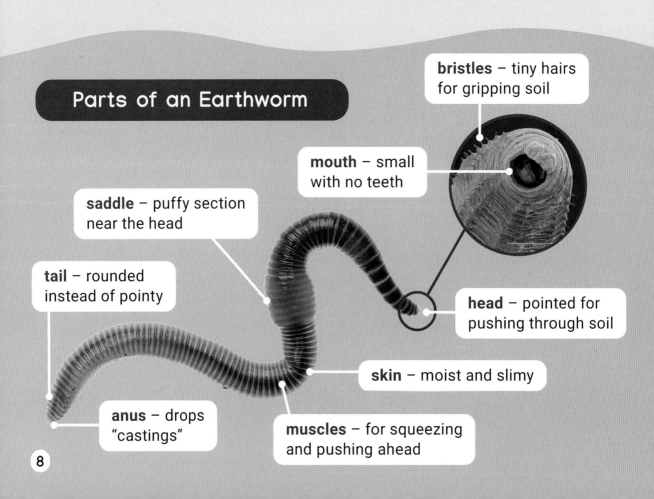

bristles – tiny hairs for gripping soil

mouth – small with no teeth

saddle – puffy section near the head

tail – rounded instead of pointy

head – pointed for pushing through soil

skin – moist and slimy

anus – drops "castings"

muscles – for squeezing and pushing ahead

Earthworms wriggle and eat their way through soil, creating long tunnels and leaving tiny spaces for the air they need to breathe. The small holes they make keep the soil loose. This lets plant roots grow long and stretch far below the surface. Also, when the soil is loose, water can trickle down to the plant roots.

an earthworm

These small creatures like to eat – a lot! Every day, earthworms gobble up many dead plants. After eating, they leave small piles of poo, called "castings". Castings are important for healthy soil. Earthworms move around and mix the castings with soil. This creates a rich layer of soil on the surface – perfect for growing plants. And it's not stinky!

Snake or Worm?

Is it a snake? No, it's a worm! The giant Gippsland earthworm from Australia is about 1 metre long. Hikers often hear them gurgling in burrows under the ground.

9

Snails and Slugs

Snails and slugs are small, soft-bodied invertebrates. They are decomposers, too.

Snails have a hard shell on their backs. They can curl their bodies and hide from predators inside their shells. They have feelers with eyes at the end. Snails have a strong jaw for tearing leaves and chewing. They creep along, leaving a slimy path.

snail

Slugs are slimy, too. They look like snails without a shell. Slugs are often found in areas that are shady or dark. They also like places that are damp.

Many snails and slugs live in gardens and compost heaps. They eat all kinds of things, like leaves from living, dying and dead plants. They also eat worms and dead insects.

slug

Snails munch on leaves in people's gardens.

Just like worms, snails and slugs make waste that is full of nutrients. This makes the soil rich and helps plants grow.

More About Snails and Slugs

→ Snails only poo once every one or two weeks!

→ At up to 30 centimetres long, the biggest slug on Earth is the ash-black slug.

→ Snails have a sort of "tongue" with microscopic teeth-like parts on it.

The teeth-like parts on a snail's tongue can be seen through a microscope.

Slaters

Slaters, sometimes called "pill bugs", are decomposers. These flat, oval-shaped invertebrates are related to lobsters. They have a hard shell made up of many **plates**, like armour!

slater

lobster

What is similar between a slater and a lobster?

Slaters eat fungi and soft, rotting plants. Sometimes they eat their own poo!

Slaters have armour-like plates on their bodies.

Slaters are shy critters that hide under bark, stones or rotting logs. Just like snails and slugs, they like damp places. If something scares them, they curl into a ball, so some people call them "roly-polies".

When a slater is threatened by a predator, like a spider, the slater curls into a ball.

In a ball, the slater is protected by its hard plates.

When a slater eats something poisonous, the poison doesn't come out in its poo. Slaters keep dangerous ingredients inside their bodies. In this way, slaters help clean up poisonous soil.

More About
Slaters

Don't let your pets eat slaters. It can make them sick.

Springtails

Like other decomposers, springtails are found in areas that are damp or wet. They live in soil, compost heaps and on the forest floor. They hide under rocks and logs.

Springtails are 1 millimetre long, so humans can see them. But it's much easier with a magnifying glass. These tiny critters have a long, soft body and six legs. The also have short **antennae** (say: *an-ten-ee*). Unlike most insects, they don't have wings. And springtails that live in soil don't have eyes. They have a spring-like part tucked under their bodies, which helps them to jump away from predators.

This is an extreme close-up of a tiny springtail.

Some springtails have scales that shimmer in the light.

Springtails work alongside other decomposers. They eat rotting plants and put back nutrients in the soil when they poo. They also eat fungi and bacteria. Some springtails eat insect poo and dead insects. All this eating helps to clean up the dead and rotting things on the ground.

More About Springtails

In early spring, people in snowy places can see a type of springtail called a snowflea. When snow begins to melt, snowfleas wiggle on the snow's surface.

Nematodes

Nematodes are another type of important decomposer. They look like tiny worms. But unlike earthworms, they don't have segments. Instead, their skin is so smooth that they are sometimes called "eel worms".

Nematodes have smooth, shiny skin.

An eel (above) is much bigger than a nematode, but they look similar.

Compost heaps have lots of nematodes. But nematodes can also survive in extreme climates. In fact, they are found all over the world. Nematodes live in Antarctica, on mountains and in the ocean. Many nematodes live in soil, near the surface.

Nematodes are hard to see because they are so small.
Some eat bacteria. Other nematodes eat fungi and
dead plants. A nematode's mouth looks like a tiny needle.

After feeding, nematodes give back rich nutrients into the soil.
Like other decomposers, nutrients are found in their waste.

It's hard to tell a nematode's head and tail apart.

The number of nematodes tells scientists about the health of the soil.

More About Nematodes

→ Nematodes live for three to seven days.

→ Imagine one rotting apple. About 90 000 nematodes could be feeding on it!

Millipedes and Centipedes

Millipedes and centipedes live all over the world, except in Antarctica. They are similar in many ways. They both like to live in moist places. Also, they both have long, segmented bodies, with antennae and lots of legs. But there are big differences between millipedes and centipedes as well.

Millipedes can be between 2.5 and 13 centimetres long. They have two pairs of legs for every one segment of their body. But centipedes can be between 1 and 30 centimetres long. Centipedes have one pair of legs for each segment of their body.

Millipedes feed on rotting plants. When they eat, they only **absorb** a small amount of nutrients. They give back the rest in their poo, which mixes with soil. This makes millipedes excellent decomposers.

A large millipede rests on a leaf.

A centipede eats an insect.

Centipedes are predators that eat other critters, such as earthworms, insects and slugs. Centipedes keep the number of other decomposers from getting too large. So scientists call centipedes decomposers, too.

More About Millipedes and Centipedes

→ The word millipede means "one thousand feet".
But they usually don't have that many.

→ Centipedes have legs that stick out, like little pointers.
Their front legs have poisonous claws to attack their prey.

Building a Mini Compost Heap

Goals

- To build a mini compost heap in a bottle
- To look for signs of decomposers at work
- To use the compost to help plants grow

Materials

a clean, empty 2-litre plastic bottle

scissors

a drill

a small plate

gardening gloves

a measuring cup

potting soil

a handful of dead leaves

a small watering can

kitchen scraps, e.g. fruit, eggshells, coffee grounds

seeds, e.g. coriander seeds

Steps

1. With an adult's help, use the scissors to cut the top off the bottle.

2. Ask an adult to use the drill to make about 10 holes in the sides and bottom of the bottle. The holes will let water drain through the soil.

3. Place the bottle on a small plate.

4. Tip 2 cups of potting soil into the bottle.

5. Sprinkle the dead leaves on top of the soil.

6. Use the watering can to add some water, to **moisten** the soil. The water will drain through the holes in the bottom and sides of the bottle.

7. Next, add the kitchen scraps. Leave a small space at the top of the bottle.

8. Put the bottle in a sunny place.

9 Water the mini compost heap every day. After four days, see how the compost has changed.

10 After a week, check for clues that decomposers are at work. Describe what you can see.

11 After four weeks, mix the compost and the soil together. This will help to add nutrients to the soil.

one week later

12 Plant some seeds.

13 Watch for signs of plant life growing in your rich soil!

Decomposers Are Important

Decomposers include bacteria, worms, springtails, millipedes and more. They have an important role in nature. They keep soil healthy and help plants grow. Without them, rotting leaves, grass clippings and dead insects would pile up. By breaking down plant waste, decomposers recycle important ingredients.

All decomposers work hard to make healthy soil.

A healthy garden needs rich soil full of decomposers.

Glossary

absorb (*verb*)	to take in
antennae (*noun*)	stalks on an insect's head (plural of antenna)
bacteria (*noun*)	tiny living things
compost heap (*noun*)	a place where plant and food scraps are put to let them break down
moist (*adjective*)	slightly wet
moisten (*verb*)	to make moist or slightly wet
moulds (*noun*)	types of fungi that are like soft fur
nutrients (*noun*)	substances that keep living things alive and healthy
plates (*noun*)	hard, flattish parts that can overlap to protect an animal's body
rich (*adjective*)	full of healthy substances
rots (*verb*)	slowly breaks down
segmented (*adjective*)	made up of connected parts, or segments
waste (*noun*)	leftover, unwanted materials

Index